Sharon Welch's
Cross-Stitch Cards

Sharon Welch's
Cross-Stitch
Cards

PREMIER
Pb
BOOKS

SHARON WELCH'S CROSS-STITCH CARDS

This edition published for
Premier Books
Mentor Business Park
Hadrian Road
Wallsend
Tyne and Wear
NE28 6HN

Art Editor LISA TAI
Editors CATHERINE WARD AND DIANA LODGE
Production ALISON MYER
Executive Editor JUDITH MORE
Art Director JACQUI SMALL

Special Photography by Debbie Patterson
Cut-outs by Clive Streeter
Illustrations by Vicky Emptage
Styling by Camilla Bambrough

ISBN 0600 582744

Produced by Mandarin Offset, Hong Kong
Printed and bound in Italy

CONTENTS

Introduction

In this section you will find basic cross-stitching instructions, including information on charting, stitching and mounting your embroidery.

We have been sending cards – for birthdays, Christmas and other special occasions – for several generations. Most cards are thrown away soon after the event, but a hand-embroidered one will be kept as a treasured keepsake for years to come:

If you are a complete beginner to cross-stitch, don't worry. The basic stitch is very simple to carry out, and with a little practice you will soon be ready to try your hand at one of the small designs in this book. When you have mounted your finished embroidery and seen the stunning result of your handiwork, you will probably feel reluctant to give it away!

These designs have all been kept to a small scale, suitable for greetings cards, but you can easily adapt them for samplers by lifting elements from several cards and combining these with an alphabet taken from the end of the book (see pp.94-95).

CROSS-STITCH TECHNIQUES
Fabric

Aida fabric with 14 holes per inch (2.5cm) was used for all the designs in this book, except for the gift tags on p.28 which were made using 16-count Aida. The amount specified takes into account the spare fabric required in order to use an embroidery hoop. If you prefer to hold the embroidery in your hand, you will require less fabric; to calculate how much you need, add a margin of 5cm (2in) to the inner frame measurements listed for each card.

Before you begin your embroidery it is a wise precaution to overcast the raw edges of the fabric using ordinary sewing thread. To make sure that your design is centered on the fabric, also mark the middle with two lines of basting stitches, one vertical and one horizontal, running from edge to edge.

Threads

Two strands of stranded embroidery cotton were used for all the cross-

Left: The basic equipment is very simple. Featured here is stranded embroidery cotton, needles, Aida cloth, scissors and a hoop.

stitching in this book, and one strand for the back-stitched outlines and lettering. You will need one skein of each colour specified in the key. As the cards are small, you will generally have ample thread for more than one card, so you may find that it is economical – with fabric as well as thread – to stitch several cards at the same time.

Working from charts

Each coloured square on the charts represents one cross-stitch, made with two strands of the appropriate colour and taken over one block of the Aida fabric. Outlines and lettering are worked in back-stitch, using one thread only in the needle.

To make it easier to follow the charts, it is often helpful to work from the middle outward. Count the maximum number of stitches horizontally and vertically and divide each in half to find the middle point. Make central horizontal and vertical lines of basting stitches across your fabric to find the middle when starting to stitch. Remove the basting stitches when you have finished the embroidery.

Using a hoop

It is possible to hold the embroidery in your hand as you stitch, but unless you have a naturally even tension the fabric will tend to become distorted with the stitches, and most people therefore prefer to use an embroidery hoop. This has two rings, one inside the other. The outer ring has either a clip or an adjustable screw so that it can be tightened to hold the fabric taut.

To stretch your fabric in the hoop, separate the rings and position the fabric centrally over the inner ring. With the tension screw loosened, place the outer ring over the fabric and the inner ring. Making sure that the fabric is smooth and evenly stretched, tighten the screw.

Cross-stitch

Stitches may be worked in horizontal rows or diagonally. When stitching large areas, work horizontally. Stitching from right to left, make a row of diagonal stitches (see fig.1). Working from left to right, go back along the row, completing each cross-stitch (see fig.2).

For diagonal lines, work downward, completing each stitch before moving to the next.

Each cross-stitch is represented by one coloured square on the chart (see fig.3). Where the chart shows a diagonal line across a square, make only one half of a cross-stitch (see fig.4).

Back-stitch

Outlines and lettering are worked in back-stitch. Make the initial stitch from right to left, then pass the needle under the fabric and bring it out one stitch length ahead, to the left of the first stitch (see fig.5); continue in this way until you have completed the outline.

French knots

This stitch is indicated on the chart by a dot. To make a French knot, bring your needle and thread out slightly to the right of the place where the knot is to be positioned. Wind the thread once or twice (for a larger knot) around the

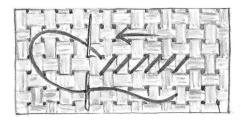

Cross-stitch (fig.1)

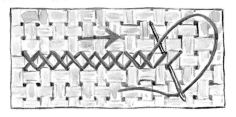

Cross-stitch (fig.2)

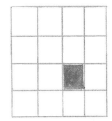

Single cross-stitch (fig.3)

Half cross-stitch (fig.4)

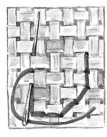

Back-stitch (fig.5)   *French knot (fig.6)*

needle, and reinsert the needle slightly to the left of the exit point (see fig.6). Gently pull the thread through the fabric, taking care to leave the knot on the surface.

Adding personal touches

You can easily personalize your card with a date, place or name, perhaps adding tiny motifs such as hearts, bows or flowers as further decorative touches. Start by drawing on graph paper the various design elements that you wish to include. Using the alphabet given on pp.94-95, write the name and other details. Cut out each of the design elements, leaving a margin of one square around each motif.

Place the designs on a fresh sheet of graph paper and move them around until you find a satisfactory arrangement. Balance is an important factor in a successful design, so make sure that your design is not top-heavy, and use the tiny fill-ins to help to balance out any unevenness. When you are happy with the design, glue the motifs and lettering in position and colour in the squares to complete your stitch chart. A colour key will help you to match your threads to colours on the graph.

Calculating the size

Unless you have used graph paper with exactly the same number of squares (stitches) per inch as the count of your fabric, your graph design will differ in size from the finished embroidery. To calculate the measurements of your embroidery, count the (maximum) number of stitches horizontally and vertically on the graph design and divide these numbers by the thread count of your fabric. For example, if you are using a 14-count Aida (in other words Aida fabric with 14 blocks/stitches per inch/2.5cm), the calculation might be as follows:

Maximum number of stitches vertically = 63
Maximum number of stitches horizontally = 77
Design size vertically: $63 \div 14 = 4\frac{1}{2}$in ($4.5 \times 2.5 = 11.25$cm)
Design size horizontally: $77 \div 14 = 5\frac{1}{2}$in ($5.5 \times 2.5 = 13.75$cm)

To the above design measurements you should add a 2in (5cm) border to allow for mounting and to leave a little space around the design. The amount of fabric required would therefore be $8\frac{1}{2}$in x $9\frac{1}{2}$in (21.5cm x 23.75cm), plus a little extra if the design is to be worked in an embroidery hoop.

MAKING THE MOUNT

Card mounts can be purchased from many craft stores and suppliers, but if you have stitched a design that will not fit a ready-made mount, there is no need to worry. It is a very simple matter to make your own card mount; all you require is thick coloured paper (available from art shops or stationers), for the mount, plus all-purpose adhesive,double-sided tape, a pencil, a ruler, a set square, a craft knife, and a blunt-ended tool, such as the back of a knife, for scoring foldlines.

The frame area

Begin by measuring the maximum height and width of the stitched area of your design. To allow a little space around the stitched area, add 2cm (¾in) to each of these measurements; this will give you the window measurement. Add a further 4cm (1½in) each way (allowing for the card frame) to find the dimensions of the front of the mount.

For example, if the stitched area measures 7.5cm x 10cm (3in x 4in); you would add 2cm (¾in), making the window area of the mount 9.5cm x 12cm (3¼in x 4¾in), and then a further 4cm (1½in), to make the front of the mount 13½cm x 16cm (5¼in x 6¼in).

To make a mount

Depending on the shape of the design, and your own preference, you might wish the card to open from either a vertical or horizontal foldline. In both cases, the window remains in the middle section. For a vertical (left-hand side) fold, take the width measurement of the frame and multiply by three. For a horizontal (top) fold, multiply the height by three. Cut your card to size. (Before cutting, it is a good idea to make sure that your corners are accurate right angles by checking that the diagonal measurements from corner to corner are the same each way.)

Score across the back of the card along the foldlines. Taking the middle (frame) section and working on the wrong side of the card, mark out the window area, measuring 2cm (¾in) in from each edge (this measurement will vary according to personal preference). Measure in a further 1cm (⅜in) and mark out an inner frame. Using a craft knife and metal ruler, carefully cut out the central, inner frame. Cut diagonally from each corner of the inner cut-out area to the corresponding corner of the marked-out window. Score along the marked window lines.

Fold back the flaps to the wrong side of the card and secure them with adhesive. Still working from the wrong side, trim 3mm (⅛in) from the left-hand side of the card, if the foldline is vertical, or cut along the bottom edge if the foldline is horizontal.

Mounting the embroidery

Press the finished embroidery lightly on the wrong side, using a steam iron. Keeping the design centered, trim the edges so that the fabric is about 1cm (⅜in) smaller all around than the frame section of the mount.

Still on the wrong side of the mount, attach a strip of double-sided tape to the inside edges of the window frame, and to the three outer edges of the front flap. Place your embroidery right-side up on a flat surface, and position the window centrally over the design. Gently press the taped window edges over the embroidery, then fold back the front flap, thus covering the wrong side of the stitching.

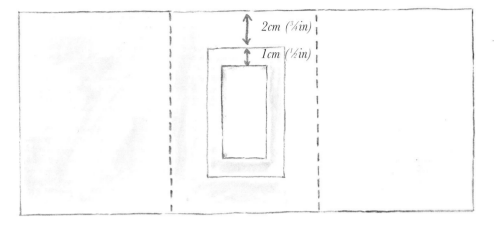

2cm (¾in)

1cm (½in)

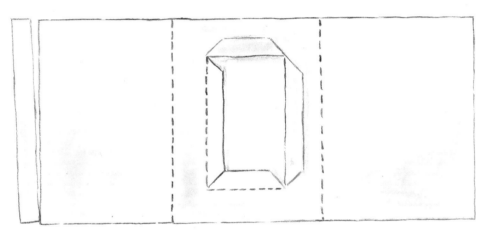

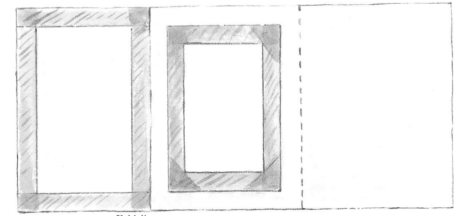

Fold line

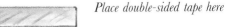

Place double-sided tape here

9

BIRTHDAYS

$\mathcal{A}$ handmade card, with a pretty cross-stitched design, is a present in itself, and would make any birthday extra special.

HAPPY BIRTHDAY

1

Congratulations on your Eighteenth Birthday

HEARTS AND FLOWERS

Finished size:

13cm (5⅛in) square

Inner frame: 9cm (3½in) square

You will need:

- 25-cm (10-in) square of white 14-count Aida
- Size 24 tapestry needle
- One skein of each colour listed in the chart
- 39cm x 13cm (15⅜in x 5⅛in) coloured cardboard
- Adhesive

NOTE: Outline in black.

	Anchor	DMC		Anchor	DMC
	403	310		239	702
	140	799		101	552
	46	666		289	307

HAPPY BIRTHDAY

Finished size:

20cm x 10.5cm (8in x 4¼in)

Inner frame: 16cm x 6.5cm (6¼in x 2½in)

You will need:

- 30cm x 20cm (12in x 8in) of white 14-count Aida
- Size 24 tapestry needle
- One skein of each colour listed in the chart
- 20cm x 31.5cm (8in x 12¾in) coloured cardboard
- Adhesive

NOTE: Outline in black.

	Anchor	DMC
■	403	310
■	25	776
■	109	209
■	140	799
■	240	966

CHEERFUL CLOWN

Finished size:

11cm x 15cm (4½in x 6in)

Inner frame: 7cm x 11cm (2¾in x 4½in)

You will need:

- 20cm x 25cm (8in x 10in) of white 14-count Aida
- Size 24 tapestry needle
- One skein of each colour listed in the chart
- 33cm x 15cm (13in x 6in) coloured cardboard
- Adhesive

NOTE: The clown's nose and the dots on his hat are made with small French knots, using black stranded cotton. Outline in black.

	Anchor	DMC		Anchor	DMC
■	403	310	■	48	963
■	46	666	■	120	3747
■	290	444	■	109	209
■	239	702	■	229	701
■	146	334			

BALLOONIST BEAR

Finished size:

11.5cm x 15cm (4½in x 6in)

Inner frame: 9cm x 12.5cm (3½in x 5in)

You will need:

• 20cm x 25cm (8in x 10in) of white 14-count Aida

• Size 24 tapestry needle

• One skein of each colour listed in the chart

• 34.5cm x 15cm (13½in x 6in) coloured cardboard

• Adhesive

NOTE: The eyes and nose, and the dots at the end of the ropes, are made with small French knots, using black stranded cotton. Outline the hearts in red and back-stitch the flower stems in light green; other outlines and lettering are in black.

	Anchor	DMC		Anchor	DMC
	403	310		225	907
	25	776		109	209
	101	552		289	307
	140	799		347	921
	229	701		371	433
	46	666			

HAPPY 1ST BIRTHDAY

Finished size:

14.5cm x 13cm (5½in x 5⅛in)

Inner frame: 10cm x 9cm (4in x 3½in)

You will need:

- 25-cm (10-in) square of white 14-count Aida
- 60cm (24in) of pink ribbon, 4mm (⅛in) wide
- Size 24 tapestry needle
- One skein of each colour listed in the chart
- 14.5cm x 39cm (5½in x 15⅜in) coloured cardboard
- Adhesive

NOTE: Back-stitch the lettering, the rabbit and the candle outlines in black, and the border in deep pink. The ribbon is secured with pale pink cross-stitches, made over two blocks of the fabric, with two blocks in between each stitch. To finish, tie a neat bow at the base and trim the ends to equal lengths. For an older child, substitute age "1" for numbers 2-6.

	Anchor	DMC			Anchor	DMC
	25	776			01	white
	28	892			398	415
	109	209			400	317
	403	310				

THE KEY TO THE DOOR

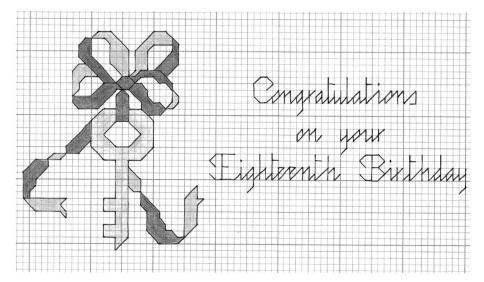

Finished size:

19.5cm x 12cm (7½in x 4¾in)

Inner frame: 15cm x 8cm (6in x 3⅛in)

You will need:

- 30cm x 20cm (12in x 8in) of white 14-count Aida
- 60cm (24in) of white lace trim, 1.5cm (½in) deep
- Size 24 tapestry needle
- One skein of each colour listed in the chart
- 19.5cm x 36cm (7½in x 14⅛in) coloured cardboard
- Adhesive

NOTE: Outline the bow in dark blue and the key in gray. Either use compasses or a circular object, such as a glass, to mark out the sides of the inner frame. Attach the lace trim using craft adhesive after making up the card.

	Anchor	DMC
■	403	310
▨	120	3747
▨	140	799
▨	133	796
▨	400	317
☐	silver thread	

21 TODAY

Finished size:

15cm (6in) square

Inner frame: 11cm (4½in) square

You will need:

- 20-cm (8-in) square of white 14-count Aida
- Size 24 tapestry needle
- One skein of each colour listed in the chart
- Adhesive
- 45cm x 15cm (18in x 6in) coloured cardboard

NOTE: Outline the glass, balloons and bottle in black, and use the photograph as a guide when back-stitching the party streamers.

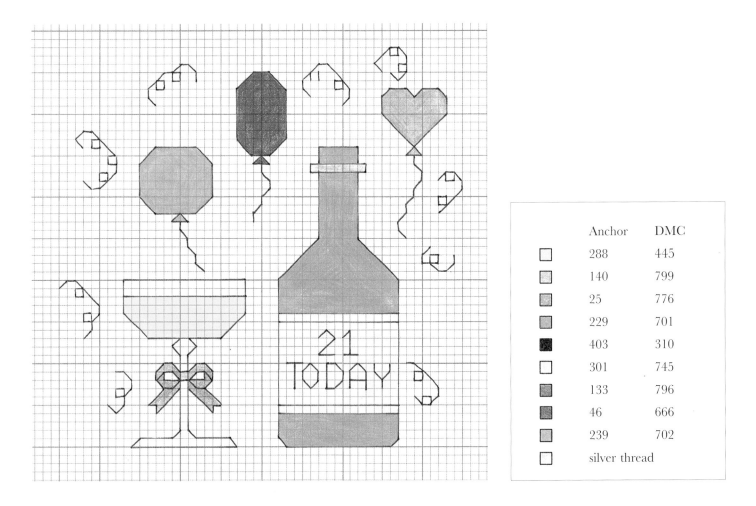

	Anchor	DMC
☐	288	445
☐	140	799
☐	25	776
☐	229	701
■	403	310
☐	301	745
☐	133	796
☐	46	666
☐	239	702
☐	silver thread	

HAPPY 40TH BIRTHDAY

Finished size:

15cm x 13cm (6in x 5⅛in)

Inner frame: 10.5cm x 9cm (4¼in x 3½in)

You will need:

- 25-cm (10-in) square of white 14-count Aida
- 4 red ribbon roses
- 8 silver leaf sequins
- 15cm (6in) of pink ribbon, 4mm (⅛in) wide
- Size 24 tapestry needle
- One skein of each colour listed in the chart
- 19.5cm x 36cm (7½in x 14¼in) coloured cardboard
- Adhesive

NOTE: Make up the card (see overleaf for chart and colour keys) and then secure the pink bow, red roses and silver leaves with craft adhesive. Outline in black.

Anchor	DMC
403	310
140	799
25	776
109	209
239	702
46	666
229	701
	silver thread

HAPPY 50TH BIRTHDAY

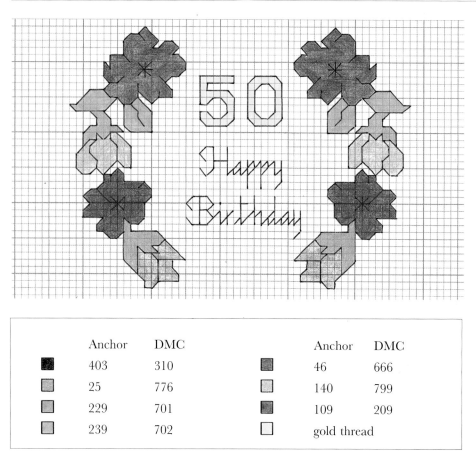

Finished size:
15.5cm x 13cm (6¼in x 5⅛in)
Inner frame: 11.5cm x 9cm (4½in x 3½in)

You will need:
• 25-cm (10-in) square of white 14-count Aida
• 50cm (20in) of white lace trim, 1.5cm (½in) deep
• Size 24 tapestry needle
• One skein of each colour listed in the chart

Anchor	DMC		Anchor	DMC
403	310		46	666
25	776		140	799
229	701		109	209
239	702			gold thread

- 15.5cm x 39cm (6¼in x 15⅜in) coloured cardboard
- Adhesive

NOTE: Outline throughout in black. Either use compasses or a circular object, such as a glass, to mark the oval of the inner frame. Attach the lace trim with craft adhesive after making up the card.

HAPPY 60TH BIRTHDAY

Finished size:

13cm x 14cm (5⅛in x 5½in)

Inner frame: 9cm x 10cm (3½in x 4in)

You will need:

- 25-cm (10-in) square of white 14-count Aida
- 28 flower-shaped silver beads, 4mm (⅛in) in diameter
- Size 24 tapestry needle
- One skein of each colour listed in the chart
- 39cm x 14cm (15⅜in x 5½in) coloured cardboard
- Adhesive

NOTE: Outline throughout in black. Either use compasses or a circular object, such as a glass, to mark out the oval shape of the inner frame. Use craft adhesive to attach the silver beads after making up the card.

	Anchor	DMC		Anchor	DMC
■	403	310	■	239	702
■	109	209	■	140	799
■	25	776	■	120	3747
□	silver thread				

CHRISTMAS

A cross-stitch card is a delightful way
of sending seasonal greetings to a friend
from whom distance has separated you.

Happy

Christmas

*On the ninth day
of Christmas my true
love sent to me*

*Happy
Christmas*

Once in Royal David's city
Stood a lowly cattle shed
Where a mother laid her baby
In a manger for his bed
Mary was that mother mild
Jesus Christ her little child

Christmas Greetings

...ish you a merry Christmas
...d a happy New Year

The holly and the Ivy
When they are both full grown
Of all the trees that are in the wood
The Holly bears the crown

Christmas Greetings

You're so sweet

HAPPY CHRISTMAS

Finished size:

12.5cm x 15cm (5in x 6in)

Inner frame: 8.5cm x 11cm (3¼in x 4½in)

You will need:

- 25-cm (10-in) square of white 14-count Aida
- Size 24 tapestry needle
- One skein of each colour listed in the chart
- 37.5cm x 15cm (15in x 6in) coloured cardboard
- Adhesive

	Anchor	DMC		Anchor	DMC
■	403	310	■	22	815
■	46	666	■	140	799
■	239	702	■	120	3747
■	25	776	□	01	white

NOTE: Outline the snowman in dark blue and the ribbon border and bows in dark red.

THE HOLLY AND THE IVY

Finished size:

20cm x 12cm (8in x 4¾in)

Inner frame: 16cm x 8cm (6¼in x 3⅛in)

You will need:

- 25cm x 20cm (10in x 8in) of white 14-count Aida
- Size 24 tapestry needle
- One skein of each colour listed in the chart
- 20cm x 36cm (8in x 14¼in) coloured cardboard
- Adhesive

The holly and the Ivy
When they are both full grown
Of all the trees that are in the wood
The Holly bears the crown.

	Anchor	DMC
■	403	310
■	47	817
■	239	702
■	22	815
■	46	666
■	229	701

NOTE: Outline the holly leaves in black, and the holly berries, ribbon and bows in deep red.

CHRISTMAS PENGUIN

Finished size:
10.5cm x 16cm (4¼in x 6¼in)
Inner frame: 6.5cm x 12cm (2½in x 4¾in)

You will need:
• 20cm x 25cm (8in x 10in) of white
  14-count Aida
• Size 24 tapestry needle
• One skein of each colour listed in the
  chart
• 31.5cm x 16cm (12¾in x 6¼in)
  coloured cardboard
• Adhesive

NOTE: Outline in black.

	Anchor	DMC		Anchor	DMC
■	403	310	■	239	702
■	46	666	■	0329	947
□	289	307	□	01	white

Christmas Greetings

I SAW THREE SHIPS

Finished size:

18.5cm x 12.5cm (7¼in x 5in)

Inner frame: 14.5cm x 8.5cm (5¾in x 3¼in)

You will need:

• 25cm x 20cm (10in x 8in) of white 14-count Aida

• Size 24 tapestry needle

• One skein of each colour listed in the chart

• 18.5cm x 37.5cm (7¼in x 15in) coloured cardboard

• Adhesive

NOTE: Outline the three ships in black stranded cotton.

	Anchor	DMC		Anchor	DMC		Anchor	DMC
	403	310		146	334		01	white
	239	702		120	3747		371	433
	46	666		0349	301			

ON THE NINTH DAY OF CHRISTMAS

Finished size:

18cm x 12cm (7in x 4¾in)

Inner frame: 14cm x 8cm (5½in x 3⅛in)

You will need:

• 25cm x 20cm (10in x 8in) of white
  14-count Aida

• Size 24 tapestry needle

• Adhesive

• One skein of each colour listed in
  the chart

• 18cm x 36cm (7in x 14¼in)
  coloured cardboard

NOTE: Outline the soldier with black,
the hearts with deep red, and the
ribbon with dark green.

	Anchor	DMC		Anchor	DMC		Anchor	DMC
	403	310		239	702		22	815
	46	666		48	963		290	444
	371	433		01	white		212	561

AT CHRISTMAS WE WILL REMEMBER

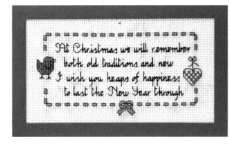

Finished size:
19cm x 12cm (7½in x 4¾in)
Inner frame:15cm x 8cm (6in x 3⅛in)
You will need:
• 25cm x 20cm (10in x 8in) of white
  14-count Aida
• Size 24 tapestry needle
• One skein of each colour listed in
  the chart
• 19cm x 36cm (7½in x 14¼in)
  coloured cardboard
• Adhesive

NOTE: Outline the robin in black, the
heart in deep red, and the ribbon in
dark green.

	Anchor	DMC		Anchor	DMC
■	403	310		212	561
	46	666		239	702
	0349	301	□	290	444
	20	498			

WE WISH YOU A MERRY CHRISTMAS

Finished size:
17cm x 12cm (6¾in x 4¾in)
Inner frame: 13cm x 8cm (5⅛in x
  3⅛in)
You will need:
• 25cm x 20cm (10in x 8in) of white
  14-count Aida
• Size 24 tapestry needle
• One skein of each colour listed in
  the chart

• Adhesive
• 17cm x 36cm (6¾in x 14¼in)
  coloured cardboard

NOTE: Outline the birds in black,
back-stitch along the tops of the snow
clumps in pale blue, and stitch the
tree in green.

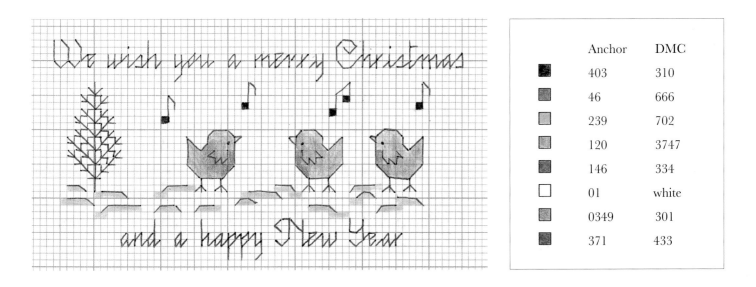

	Anchor	DMC
	403	310
	46	666
	239	702
	120	3747
	146	334
	01	white
	0349	301
	371	433

ONCE IN ROYAL DAVID'S CITY

Finished size:

18.5cm x 14cm (7¼in x 5½in)

Inner frame: 14cm x 10.5cm (5½in x 4¼in)

You will need:

- 25cm x 20cm (10in x 8in) of white 14-count Aida
- 60cm (24in) of green ribbon, 3mm (⅛in) wide
- Size 24 tapestry needle
- One skein of each colour listed in the chart
- 55.5cm x 14cm (21¾in x 5½in) coloured cardboard
- Adhesive

NOTE: The ribbon border is attached with cross-stitches made over two Aida blocks; leave one Aida block between each stitch. To finish, tie the ribbon in a neat bow at the base.

	Anchor	DMC
	403	310
	229	701

CHRISTMAS TAGS

Finished size of each tag:

5cm (2in) square

Inner frame: 3.5cm (1½in) square

For each tag, you will need:

- 5-cm (2-in) square of white 16-count Aida

- Size 24 tapestry needle
- One skein of each colour listed in the chart
- 15cm x 5cm (6in x 2in) coloured cardboard
- Adhesive

NOTE: These small tags would make ideal projects for novice cross-stitchers. To make the inner shape of the mount, either use a pair of compasses or draw around the base of a circular object, such as a small tea cup.

	Anchor	DMC		Anchor	DMC		Anchor	DMC
	46	666		403	310		140	799
	239	702		22	815			

RELIGIOUS OCCASIONS

A handmade card shows just how much you have been thinking of the recipient as an important day approaches.

Easter

Celebrate Easter and the joys of spring with a charming hand-embroidered card on a traditional theme.

EASTER PARADE

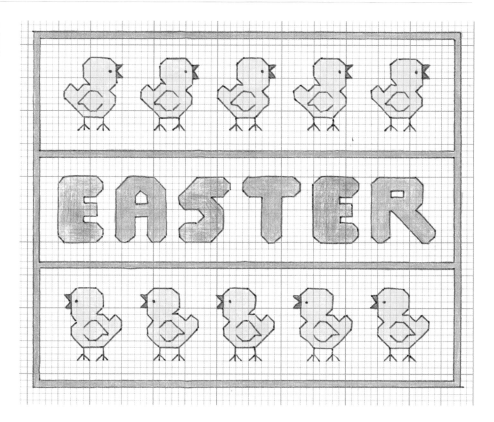

Finished size:

19cm x 16cm (7½in x 6¼in)
Inner frame: 15cm x 12cm (6in x 4¾in)

You will need:

• 30cm x 25cm (12in x 10in) of white 14-count Aida
• Size 24 tapestry needle
• One skein of each colour listed in the chart
• 19cm x 48cm (7½in x 18¾in) coloured cardboard
• Adhesive

Note: The eyes are made with small French knots, using black stranded cotton. Outline in black.

	Anchor	DMC		Anchor	DMC
■	403	310	▨	140	799
□	290	444	▨	25	776
▨	239	702	▨	0329	947

EASTER WISHES

Finished size:

17cm x 14cm (6¾in x 5½in)

Inner frame: 13cm x 10cm (5⅛in x 4in)

You will need:

- 30cm x 25cm (12in x 10in) of white 14-count Aida
- Size 24 tapestry needle
- One skein of each colour listed in the chart
- 17cm x 42cm (6¾in x 16½in) coloured cardboard
- Adhesive

NOTE: The chickens' eyes are made with small French knots, using black stranded cotton. The hearts which border the card are outlined in pink or purple, as appropriate; the blue flowers are outlined in blue and the red flowers are outlined in red from the stems up to the tip of the petals, but not at the open end of each flower. The flower stems are back-stitched in green; while the leaves are made by taking a diagonal stitch over two Aida blocks, followed by a

	Anchor	DMC		Anchor	DMC
■	403	310	☐	239	702
☐	288	445	■	46	666
■	0329	947	■	20	498
■	146	334	■	109	209
☐	130	809	■	25	776

vertical or horizontal stitch (depending on the desired angle of the leaf) across the middle of the diagonal, and then outlining the leaf shape in green.

The lettering and the three chicken outlines are in black back-stitching, and the border outlines are stitched in deep red.

YOU'RE EGGSTRA SPECIAL

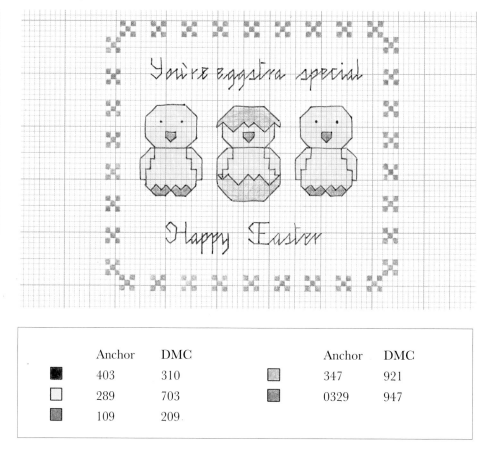

Finished size:

15cm x 14.5cm (6in x 5¾in)

Inner frame: 11cm x 10.5cm (4½in x 4¼in)

You will need:

- 25-cm (10-in) square of white 14-count Aida
- Size 24 tapestry needle
- One skein of each colour listed in the chart
- 45cm x 14.5cm (18in x 5¾in) coloured cardboard
- Adhesive

	Anchor	DMC		Anchor	DMC
■	403	310	■	347	921
□	289	703	■	0329	947
■	109	209			

NOTE: The chicks' eyes are created with small French knots, using black stranded cotton. Outline the chicks in black.

HAPPY EASTER

Finished size:

13cm x 12cm (5⅛in x 4¾in)

Inner frame: 9cm x 8cm (3½in x 3⅛in)

You will need:

- 25-cm (10-in) square of white 14-count Aida
- Size 24 tapestry needle

- One skein of each colour listed in the chart
- 13cm x 36cm (5⅛in x 14¼in) coloured cardboard
- Adhesive

NOTE: The rabbits' eyes are created with small French knots, using black stranded cotton. The lettering and the two rabbit outlines are in black back-stitching, the bow is outlined in deep red, the flower stems are stitched with green, and the inner edge of the blue cross-stitching at the top and the bottom of the egg is defined with blue back-stitching.

	Anchor	DMC
■	403	310
□	347	921
□	140	799
□	239	702
□	25	776
□	46	666
□	22	815

EASTER BLESSINGS

Finished size:
12.5cm x 14.5cm (5in x 5¾in)
Inner frame: 8.5cm x 10.5cm (3¼in x 4¼in)

You will need:
• 25-cm (10-in) square of white 14-count Aida
• Size 24 tapestry needle
• One skein of each colour listed in the chart
• 37.5cm x 14.5cm (15in x 5¾in) coloured cardboard
• Adhesive

NOTE: The lettering, purple flowers and cross are outlined in black, the bow in deep pink, and the heart and border in blue. To make the leaves, refer to Note on p.33 for instructions.

	Anchor	DMC		Anchor	DMC		Anchor	DMC
■	403	310	□	25	776	□	101	552
□	289	307	□	28	892	□	146	334
□	239	702	□	398	415	□	140	799

First Communion & Christening

Christening and first communion are two important stages in the spiritual development of a child, so mark each of these events with a special card.

FIRST COMMUNION

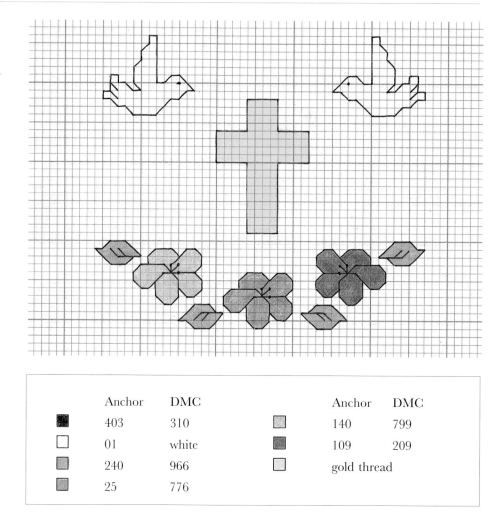

Finished size:

13.5cm x 17.5cm (5¼in x 7in)

Inner frame: 9cm x 13cm (3½in x 5⅛in)

You will need:

• 20cm x 25cm (8in x 10in) of white 14-count Aida

• Size 24 tapestry needle

• One skein of each colour listed in the chart

• 13.5cm x 52.5cm (5¼in x 20¾in) coloured cardboard

• Adhesive

	Anchor	DMC		Anchor	DMC
■	403	310		140	799
□	01	white	■	109	209
	240	966		gold thread	
	25	776			

NOTE: Outline throughout in black. Copy the general style of the inner window frame, altering it if you wish. You will find it easier to cut this card accurately if you first draw the shape of the inner frame onto the wrong side of the piece of cardboard (middle section); cut out the design using a sharp craft knife or scalpel, and then fold the card along one edge and cut the outer, curved shape through all three layers at once.

CHRISTENING

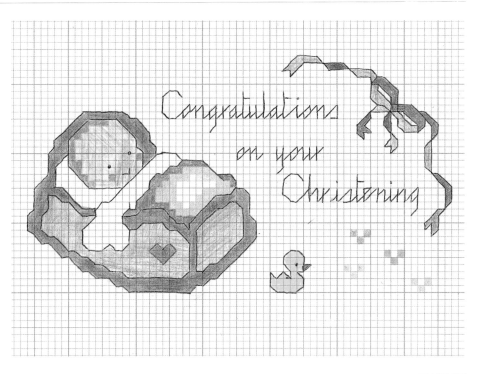

Finished size:

17cm x 12cm (6¾in x 4¾in)

Inner frame: 13cm x 8cm (5⅛in x 3⅛in)

You will need:

- 20cm x 15cm (8in x 6in) of white 14-count Aida
- Size 24 tapestry needle
- One skein of each colour listed in the chart
- 17cm x 36cm (6¾in x 14¼in) coloured cardboard
- Adhesive

NOTE: Work the cross-stitching first, then the back-stitching. The eyes are made with small French knots, using black stranded cotton. Outline in black. If you are making the card for a girl, you could change the colour of the crib cover to pink.

	Anchor	DMC		Anchor	DMC
	109	209		203	954
	103	211		120	3747
	403	310		146	334
	290	444		0329	947
	48	963		01	white
	25	776		0349	301
	347	921			

Other Religious Festivals

A light to guide the world – whether the festival is Jewish or Hindu, the message here is the same.

SHALOM

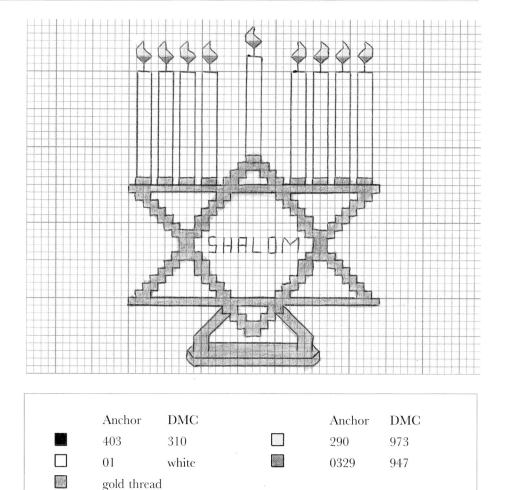

Finished size:

12.5cm x 14.5cm (5in x 5¾in)
Inner frame: 8.5cm x 10.5cm (3¼in x 4⅛in)

You will need:

• 20-cm (10-in) square of white 14-count Aida
• Size 24 tapestry needle
• One skein of each colour listed in the chart
• 37.5cm x 14.5cm (15in x 5¾in) coloured cardboard
• Adhesive

	Anchor	DMC		Anchor	DMC
■	403	310	□	290	973
□	01	white	▨	0329	947
▨	gold thread				

NOTE: For the candle flames, make three straight stitches in orange, radiating out from the bottom of the flame, and then one yellow cross-stitch and two straight yellow stitches; outline in black.

DIWALI

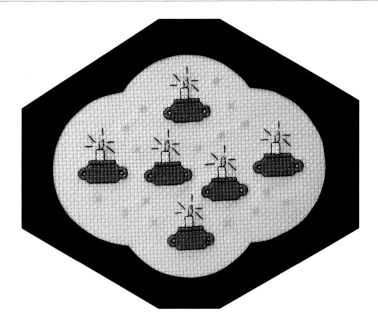

Finished size:

18.5cm x 15.5cm (7¼in x 6¼in)

Inner frame: 14cm x 11cm (5½in x 4½in)

You will need:

- 30cm x 25cm (12in x 10in) of cream 14-count Aida
- Size 24 tapestry needle
- One skein of each colour listed in the chart
- 18.5cm x 46.5cm (7¼in x 18¼in) coloured cardboard
- Adhesive

NOTE: Outline throughout in black. The card is hinged from the top edge. To make the inner shape, draw four overlapping circles on the back of the card, using a pencil and compasses or a round object, such as a glass.

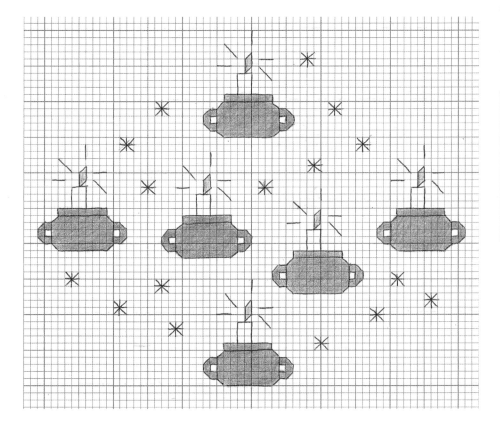

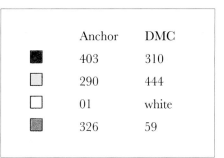

	Anchor	DMC
■	403	310
▫	290	444
□	01	white
▨	326	59

50

With love on your Wedding Day

Without love and understanding
a marriage will never be
A marriage needs tenderness
laughter and loyalty
Forgiveness, faith and happiness
are things that must be there
As well as hope and friendship
and special things you'll share
Life will be full of caring
helping each other through
For two very special people
this message is for you

WEDDINGS AND ANNIVERSARIES

Send a special memento to celebrate a wedding or anniversary – it will be cherished by the couple for years to come.

Ruby Wedding

Happy Anniversary

Pearl Anniversary

Weddings

If you truly care about the happy couple, an embroidered card is a very personal way of sending your love and good wishes on their wedding day.

WITH LOVE ON YOUR WEDDING DAY

Finished size:

14.5cm (5¾in) square

Inner frame: 9.5cm (3½in) in
   diameter

You will need:

- 20-cm (8-in) square of white
  14-count Aida
- 34cm (13½in) of pre-gathered white
  lace trim, 2cm (¾in) deep
- Size 24 tapestry needle
- One skein of each colour listed in
  the chart
- 14.5cm x 43.5cm (5¾in x 17¼in)
  coloured cardboard
- Adhesive

	Anchor	DMC		Anchor	DMC
■	403	310	■	46	666
■	140	799	■	20	498
■	120	3747	■	290	444
■	158	828			

NOTE: Outline in black. To mark out the inner frame, either use compasses or a circular object, such as a saucer or a cup. Before assembling the card, attach the lace trim with craft adhesive.

THE HAPPY COUPLE

Finished size:

20cm x 12cm (8in x 4¾in)

Inner frame: 17.5cm x 10cm (7in x 4in)

You will need:

• 30cm x 20cm (12in x 8in) of white
  14-count Aida

• Size 24 tapestry needle

• Adhesive

• One skein of each colour listed in
  the chart

• 20cm x 36cm (8in x 14¼in) coloured
  cardboard

NOTE: Outline the figures in black and
stitch the archway in green. Finish with
French knots for the eyes and buttons.

	Anchor	DMC		Anchor	DMC		Anchor	DMC
■	403	310	▤	140	799	▨	0349	301
▨	239	702	▨	398	415	□	289	307
▨	25	776	▨	46	666	▨	109	209
▨	48	963	□	01	white			

WITHOUT LOVE AND UNDERSTANDING

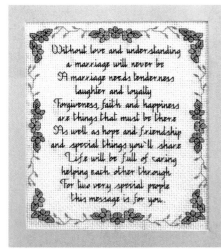

Finished size:

18.5cm x 20cm (7¼in x 8in)

Inner frame: 15cm x 17cm (6in x 6¾in)

You will need:

- 30-cm (12-in) square of white 14-count Aida
- Size 24 tapestry needle
- One skein of each colour listed in the chart
- 55.5cm x 20cm (21¾in x 8in) coloured cardboard
- Adhesive

NOTE: Work the cross-stitching first, then the back-stitching. Outline the flowers and the leaves in black; and the trailing ivy border in green.

	Anchor	DMC		Anchor	DMC
■	403	310	■	25	776
■	239	702	■	140	799

Anniversaries

Mark the important wedding anniversaries with a cross-stitched card, to keep romance alive.

WITH LOVE ON YOUR WEDDING ANNIVERSARY

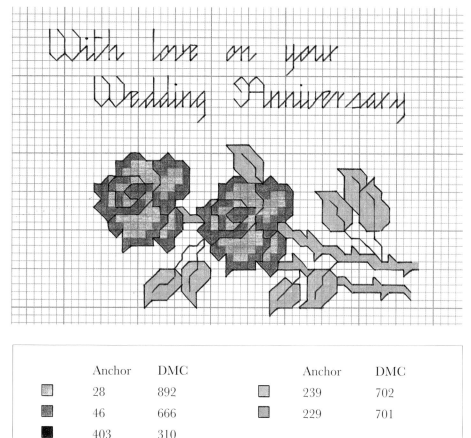

Finished size:

16cm (6¼in) square

Inner frame:12cm (4¾in) in diameter

You will need:

• 25-cm (10-in) square of white 14-count Aida

• 40cm (16in) of white lace trim, 1.5cm (½in) deep

• Size 24 tapestry needle

• One skein of each colour listed in the chart

• 16cm x 48cm (6¼in x 18¾in) coloured cardboard

• Adhesive

	Anchor	DMC		Anchor	DMC
	28	892		239	702
	46	666		229	701
	403	310			

NOTE: Outline in black. To mark out the inner frame, either use a pair of compasses or draw around a circular object, such as a saucer or a large cup. Attach the lace border with craft adhesive before assembling the card.

SILVER ANNIVERSARY

Finished size:

16.5cm x 19.5cm (6½in x 7¾in)

Inner frame:13.5cm x 16.5cm (5¼in x 6½in)

You will need:

- 30-cm (12-in) square of white 14-count Aida
- 62 silver beads, 4mm (⅛in) in diameter
- Silver "25" cake decoration, 2cm (¾in) high
- White sewing cotton and needle
- Size 24 tapestry needle
- One skein of each colour listed in the chart
- 49.5cm x 19.5cm (19½in x 7¾in) coloured cardboard
- Adhesive

NOTE: Outline pink bow with red, blue bow with dark blue, and bells with dark gray. Stitch bell bands in pale green. When you have finished cross-stitching, sew the beads in place, then assemble the card. Finally, glue on the decoration.

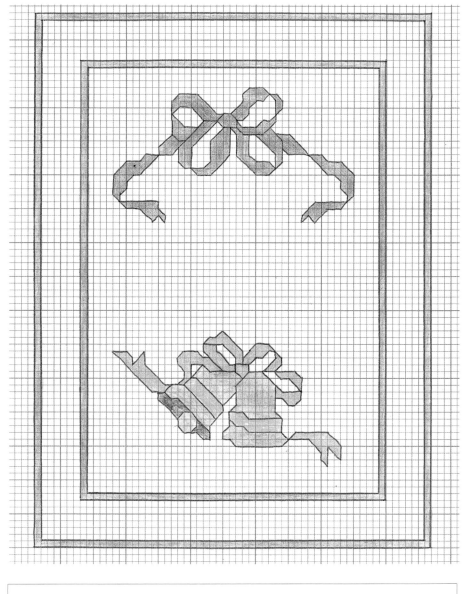

	Anchor	DMC		Anchor	DMC
	25	776		398	415
	28	892		400	317
	120	3747		206	966
	146	334		silver thread	

46

PEARL ANNIVERSARY

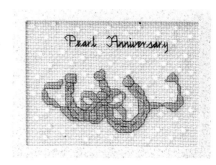

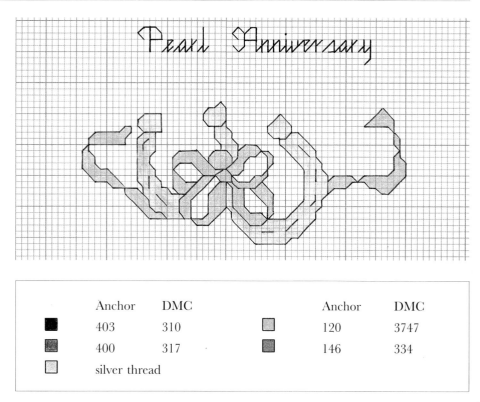

Finished size:

14cm x 10.5cm (5½in x 4¼in)

Inner frame: 12cm x 8.5cm (4¾in x 3¼in)

You will need:

- 25cm x 20cm (10in x 8in) of white
  14-count Aida
- 60 small pearl beads
- White sewing cotton and needle
- Size 24 tapestry needle
- One skein of each colour listed in
  the chart
- 42cm x 10.5cm (16½in x 4¼in)
  coloured cardboard
- Adhesive

	Anchor	DMC		Anchor	DMC
■	403	310	□	120	3747
▨	400	317	▨	146	334
□	silver thread				

NOTE: Outline the blue bow with dark blue, and the horseshoes with gray. Stitch the pearl beads in position before assembling the card.

HAPPY ANNIVERSARY

Finished size:

20cm x 11cm (8in x 4½in)

Inner frame:16cm x 7cm (6¼in x 2¾in)

You will need:

- 25cm x 15cm (10in x 6in) of white
  14-count Aida
- 55cm (22in) of white lace trim,
  1.5cm (½in) deep
- Silver bells cake decoration, 2cm
  (¾in) high
- White sewing cotton and needle

- Size 24 tapestry needle
- One skein of each colour listed in
  the chart
- 20cm x 33cm (8in x 13in) coloured
  cardboard
- Adhesive

NOTE: Outline the ribbon with dark blue, and the doves with gray. Glue the lace in place before assembling the card. (For chart and key, see overleaf.)

	Anchor	DMC
■	400	317
□	01	white
▨	120	3747
▨	146	334

RUBY ANNIVERSARY

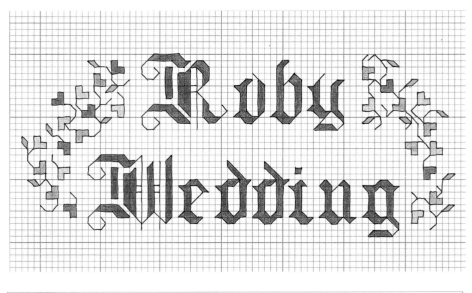

Finished size:

22cm x 13cm (8½in x 6¼in)

Inner frame:16cm x 7cm (6in x 2¾in)

You will need:

- 30cm x 20cm (12in x 8in) of white 14-count Aida
- 70cm (27¼in) of white lace trim, 3cm (1¼in) deep
- 70cm (27¼in) of red ribbon, 6mm (¼in) wide
- 4 red ribbon roses
- Size 24 tapestry needle
- One skein of each colour listed in the chart
- 22cm x 39cm (8½in x 15⅜in) coloured cardboard
- Adhesive

	Anchor	DMC		Anchor	DMC
■	46	666	▨	109	209
▨	140	799	▨	239	702
▨	25	776			

NOTE: To make up the border, thread a piece of narrow red ribbon through the white lace edging and attach it to the cardboard with craft adhesive, making sure that you mitre the corners neatly to fit exactly. After assembling the card, glue the red ribbon roses into position.

GOLDEN ANNIVERSARY

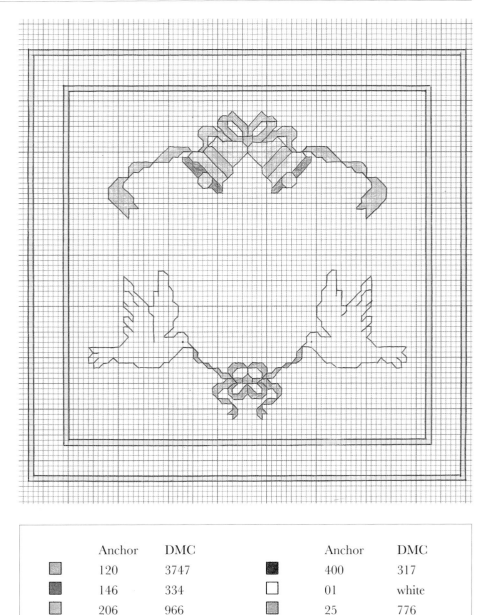

Finished size:

22cm x 20cm (8½in x 8in)

Inner frame:18cm x 16.5cm (7in x 6½in)

You will need:

- 30-cm (12-in) square of white 14-count Aida
- 78 flower-shaped gold beads, 4mm (⅛in) in diameter
- Gold "50" cake decoration, 2.5cm (1in) high
- White sewing cotton and needle
- Size 24 tapestry needle
- One skein of each colour listed in the chart
- 66cm x 20cm (25½in x 8in) coloured cardboard
- Adhesive

NOTE: Outline the pink bow in red, the blue bow in dark blue, and the bells and doves in gray. Cross-stitch the bell bands in pale green. Once you have finished cross-stitching, sew the individual flower-shaped beads into position around the border using white sewing cotton. Next, assemble the card and glue the gold "50" cake decoration in the middle of the design with craft adhesive.

	Anchor	DMC		Anchor	DMC
	120	3747		400	317
	146	334		01	white
	206	966		25	776
	398	415		28	892
	gold thread			silver thread	

49

BABIES

If you give your card with a pretty frame, it can be kept and used to decorate baby's bedroom.

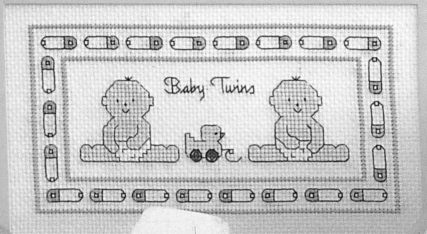

Baby Twins

Welcome

Greet a new member of the family with one of these delightful cards, which will be treasured for years to come.

BOY OR GIRL?

Finished size:
19.5cm x 16.5cm (7½in x 6½in)
Inner frame: 15.5cm x 12.5cm (6¼in x 5in)

You will need:
- 30cm x 25cm (12in x 10in) of white 14-count Aida
- Size 24 tapestry needle
- Adhesive

- One skein of each colour listed in the chart
- 19.5cm x 49.5cm (7½in x 19½in) coloured cardboard

NOTE: The eyes are made with French knots, using black stranded cotton. Outline in black, except for the bows, which are in deep pink and deep blue.

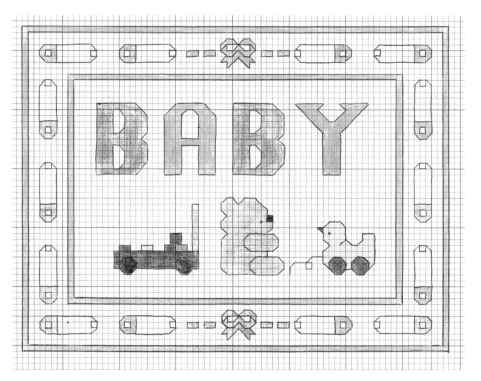

	Anchor	DMC
	403	310
	46	666
	225	912
	140	799
	25	776
	28	892
	133	796
	347	921
	290	444
	0329	947
	101	552
	398	415
	229	701

TWINS

Finished size:

23.5cm x 14.5cm (9¼in x 5¾in)

Inner frame: 19.5cm x 10.5cm (7½in
x 4¼in)

You will need:

• 30cm x 25cm (12in x 10in) of white
14-count Aida

• Size 24 tapestry needle

• One skein of each colour listed in
the chart

• 23.5cm x 43.5cm (9¼in x 17¼in)
coloured cardboard

• Adhesive

NOTE: The eyes are made with small
French knots, using black stranded
cotton. Outline in black.

	Anchor	DMC
	403	310
	242	913
	46	666
	25	776
	289	307
	01	white
	48	963
	0329	947
	140	799

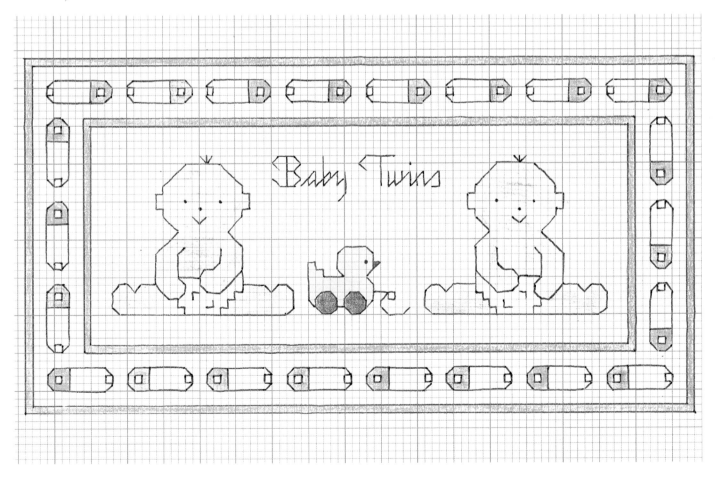

BABY GIRL

Finished size:

20cm x 13.5cm (8in x 5¼in)

Inner frame: 16cm x 9.5cm (6¼in x 3¼in)

You will need:

- 30cm x 25cm (12in x 10in) of white 14-count Aida
- Size 24 tapestry needle
- One skein of each colour listed in the chart
- 20cm x 40.5cm (8in x 16in) coloured cardboard
- Adhesive

NOTE: Complete the cross-stitching first, then work the back-stitching. The eyes are created with small French knots, using black stranded cotton. Outline throughout in black, except for the ribbon which is stitched in dark red.

	Anchor	DMC		Anchor	DMC
■	403	310	□	398	415
▨	46	666	▨	140	799
▨	347	921	□	290	444
▨	239	702	▨	0329	947
▨	25	776	▨	103	211
▨	20	498			

BABY BOY

Finished size:

19cm x 13cm (7½in x 5⅛in)

Inner frame: 15cm x 9cm (6in x 3½in)

You will need:

- 30cm x 25cm (12in x 10in) of white 14-count Aida
- Size 24 tapestry needle
- Adhesive
- One skein of each colour listed in the chart
- 19cm x 39cm (7½in x 15⅜in) coloured cardboard

NOTE: The eyes are made with small French knots, using black stranded cotton. Outline in black.

	Anchor	DMC
■	403	310
■	239	702
□	01	white
■	0349	301
■	289	307
■	146	334
■	25	776
■	130	809
■	46	666
■	22	815
■	229	701

STORK

Finished size:

15.5cm (6¼in) between opposite
   points
Inner frame: 8.5cm (3¼in) between
   opposite points

You will need:

- 20-cm (10-in) square of white
   14-count Aida
- 35cm (14in) of white lace edging,
   12mm (½in) wide
- 6 small pale-blue ribbon bows
- Size 24 tapestry needle
- One skein of each colour listed in
   the chart
- 15.5cm x 46.5cm (6¼in x 18¼in)
   coloured cardboard
- Adhesive

NOTE: The eye is made with a small
French knot, using black stranded
cotton. If you are making the card for
a girl, you could substitute pink card
and bows for blue, and use a deep
pink for the shawl. Outline in black.

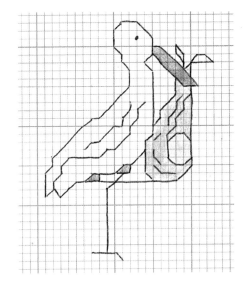

	Anchor	DMC		Anchor	DMC
□	01	white	■	120	3747
■	0329	947	■	48	963
■	403	310			

SPECIAL OCCASIONS

*S*urprise a loved one with a handmade card to say
"Get well" or "I love you", or to celebrate a special day.

St Valentine's Day

Now is the perfect time to stitch a romantic keepsake for your nearest and dearest.

JUST BECAUSE I LOVE YOU

Finished size:

14cm x 12cm (5½in x 4¾in)

Inner frame: 10cm x 8cm (4in x 3⅛in)

You will need:

- 25-cm (10-in) square of white 14-count Aida
- Size 24 tapestry needle
- One skein of each colour listed in the chart
- 14cm x 36cm (5½in x 14¼in) coloured cardboard
- Adhesive

NOTE: The bear's eyes are made with small French knots, using black stranded cotton. Outline in black.

	Anchor	DMC		Anchor	DMC
	403	310		46	666
	25	776		347	921
	239	702		349	301
	140	799			

TO MY SWEETHEART ON VALENTINE'S DAY

Finished size:

16cm (6¼in) square

Inner frame: 12cm (4¾in) square

You will need:

- 25-cm (10-in) square of white
  14-count Aida
- Size 24 tapestry needle
- One skein of each colour listed in
  the chart
- 16cm x 48cm (6¼in x 18¾in)
  coloured cardboard
- Adhesive

NOTE: Complete the cross-stitching first, then work the back-stitching. The bow at the top of the heart is outlined in dark red; and the ribbon holding the miniature heart is back-stitched in gray.

	Anchor	DMC		Anchor	DMC
■	403	310	■	46	666
■	47	304	■	22	815
■	239	702	■	400	317
□	01	white	■	140	799
■	25	776			

HAPPY VALENTINE'S DAY

- One skein of each colour listed in the chart
- 26cm x 43.5cm (10¼in x 17¼in) coloured cardboard
- 4 red ribbon roses
- 78cm (30¾in) of white and red lace trim, 2cm (¾in) wide
- 8cm (3¼in) of red ribbon, 3mm (⅛in) wide
- Adhesive

Finished size:

26cm x 14.5cm (10¼in x 5¾in)

Inner frame: 20cm x 8.5cm (8in x 3¼in)

You will need:

- 26cm x 14.5cm (10¼in x 5¾in) of white 14-count Aida
- Size 24 tapestry needle

NOTE: Work the cross-stitching first, then the back-stitching. Outline the blue ribbon border in dark blue, and the hearts in red.

	Anchor	DMC		Anchor	DMC		Anchor	DMC
■	403	310	■	133	796	■	25	776
■	140	799	■	46	666	■	229	701

Mother's & Father's Day

An embroidered card for Mother's or Father's Day will be treasured long after flowers have been thrown away.

HAPPY MOTHER'S DAY

Finished size:

12cm x 11.5cm (4¾in x 4½in)

Inner frame: 9.5cm x 9cm (3½in x 3½in)

You will need:

- 25-cm (10-in) square of white 14-count Aida
- Size 24 tapestry needle
- One skein of each colour listed in the chart
- 36cm x 11.5cm (14¼in x 4½in) coloured cardboard
- Adhesive

NOTE: The stamens are made with small French knots, using black stranded cotton. Outline in black; the white flower and the white bands on the bowl are cross-stitched in white.

	Anchor	DMC		Anchor	DMC
■	403	310	■	146	334
▨	25	776	□	289	307
▨	140	799	▨	0329	947
▨	229	701	■	20	498
▨	46	666	▨	109	209
□	01	white			

WITH LOVE TO A VERY SPECIAL MUM

Finished size:

16.5cm x 17.5cm (6½in x 7in)

Inner frame: 12.5cm x 13.5cm (5in x
5¼in)

You will need:

- 30-cm (12-in) square of white
  14-count Aida
- Size 24 tapestry needle
- One skein of each colour listed in
  the chart
- 49.5cm x 17.5cm (19½in x 7in)
  coloured cardboard
- Adhesive

NOTE: The bear's eyes are created
with small French knots, using black
stranded cotton. Outline the four
bows in deep lilac and the red flower
in red; the flower stems are back-
stitched in green, and all other outlines are black.

	Anchor	DMC		Anchor	DMC
■	403	310		239	702
	347	921		25	776
	46	666		101	552
	229	701		109	209
	140	799			

FOR DAD

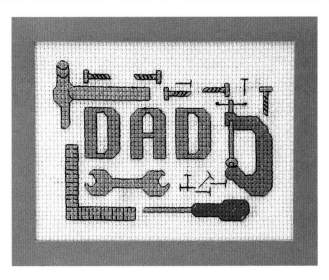

- One skein of each colour listed in the chart
- 16cm x 39cm (6¼in x 15⅜in) coloured cardboard
- Adhesive

NOTE: Outline throughout in black stranded cotton.

	Anchor	DMC
	403	310
	239	702
	398	415
	46	666
	146	334
	367	738

Finished size:

16cm x 13cm (6¼in x 5⅛in)

Inner frame: 12cm x 9cm (4¾in x 3½in)

You will need:

- 25-cm (10-in) square of white 14-count Aida
- Size 24 tapestry needle

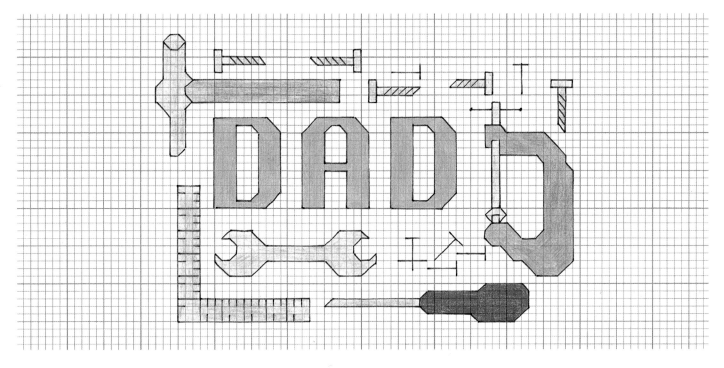

Halloween

No child could resist these spooky cards, complete with pumpkins, spiders, and the inevitable bats.

WICKED WITCH

Finished size:

15.5cm x 12cm (6¼in x 4¾in)

Inner frame: 11.5cm x 8cm (4½in x 3⅛in)

You will need:

- 25cm x 20cm (10in x 8in) of white 14-count Aida
- Size 24 tapestry needle
- One skein of each colour listed in the chart
- 46.5cm x 12cm (18¼in x 4¾in) coloured cardboard
- Adhesive

NOTE: The witch's and cat's eyes are made with small French knots, using black stranded cotton. Outline throughout in black.

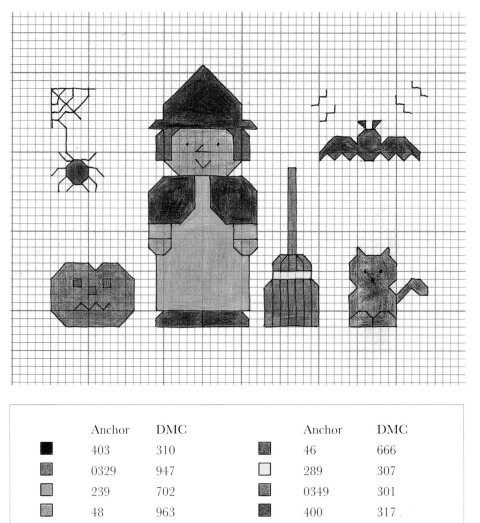

	Anchor	DMC		Anchor	DMC
	403	310		46	666
	0329	947		289	307
	239	702		0349	301
	48	963		400	317

GHOST PARTY

- Size 24 tapestry needle
- One skein of each colour listed in the chart
- 24cm x 34.5cm (9½in x 13½in) coloured cardboard
- Adhesive

NOTE: The eyes are all made with small French knots, using black stranded cotton. Outline in black; the ghosts are shaded with white cross-stitches.

Finished size:
24cm x 11.5cm (9½in x 4½in)
Inner frame: 20cm x 7.5cm (8in x 3in)

You will need:
- 35cm x 20cm (14in x 8in) of white 14-count Aida

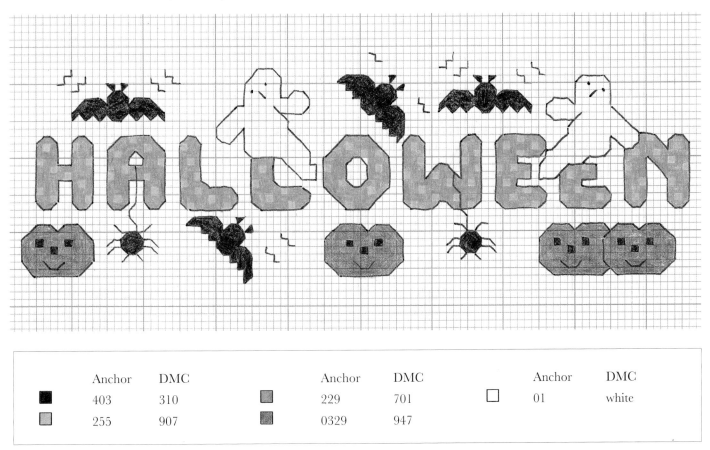

	Anchor	DMC		Anchor	DMC		Anchor	DMC
■	403	310	■	229	701	□	01	white
■	255	907	■	0329	947			

GENERAL GREETINGS

There are numerous occasions when an embroidered card can show how much you think about your friends and loved ones – in good times and in bad.

Personal Messages

Here are a few cheering greetings cards that will be useful for many special occasions.

SPECIAL DAY CARD

Finished size:

15.5cm x 11.5cm (6¼in x 4½in)
Inner frame: 13cm x 9cm (5⅛in x 3½in)

You will need:

- 25cm x 20cm (10in x 8in) of white 14-count Aida
- Size 24 tapestry needle
- One skein of each colour listed in the chart
- 15.5cm x 35cm (6¼in x 14in) coloured cardboard
- Adhesive

NOTE: Work the cross-stitching first, then the back-stitching. The bird's eye is created with a small French knot, using black stranded cotton. Outline in black.

	Anchor	DMC		Anchor	DMC
	403	310		25	776
	46	666		229	701
	0349	301		398	415
	289	307		47	304
	239	702		109	209

PRIMROSES

Finished size:

17cm x 22cm (6¾in x 8½in)

Inner frame: 13cm x 18cm (5⅛in x 7in)

You will need:

- 25cm x 30cm (10in x 12in) of white 14-count Aida
- Size 24 tapestry needle
- One skein of each colour listed in the chart
- 51cm x 22cm (20¼in x 8½in) coloured cardboard
- Adhesive

NOTE: Outline in black.

	Anchor	DMC		Anchor	DMC		Anchor	DMC
	403	310		289	307		101	552
	140	799		239	702		398	415
	146	334		229	701		347	921
	0349	301		47	304			
	46	666		0329	947			

Children's Alphabet

Create a personal message for your child using these fun letters. If you give the card with a frame you could mount it and attach it to the bedroom door.

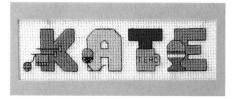 

	Anchor	DMC
	01	white
	290	444
	0329	947
	46	666
	20	498
	48	963
	109	209
	99	552
	146	334
	161	3760
	239	702
	229	701
	0349	301
	347	921
	398	415
	400	317
	403	310

Finished size for Kate:
16cm x 6.5cm (6¼in x 2½in)
Inner frame: 13.5cm x 4cm (5¼in x 1½in)

You will need:
- 25cm x 10cm (10in x 4in) of white 14-count Aida
- Size 24 tapestry needle
- One skein of each colour listed in the chart
- 16cm x 19.5cm (6¼in x 7½in) coloured cardboard
- Adhesive

NOTE: To make up, follow the chart given below. Outline in black.

Finished size for Tim:
15.5cm x 8cm (6¼in x 3⅛in)
Inner frame: 11.5cm x 4cm (4½in x 1½in)

You will need:
- 20cm x 10cm (8in x 4in) of white 14-count Aida
- Size 24 tapestry needle
- One skein of each colour listed in the chart
- 15.5cm x 24cm (6¼in x 9½in) coloured cardboard
- Adhesive

NOTE: To make up, follow the chart given on p.71. Outline in black.

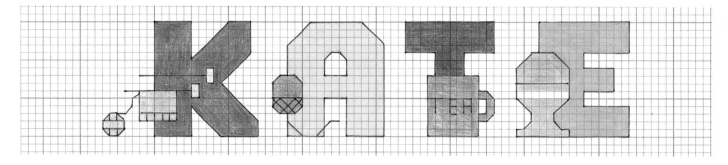

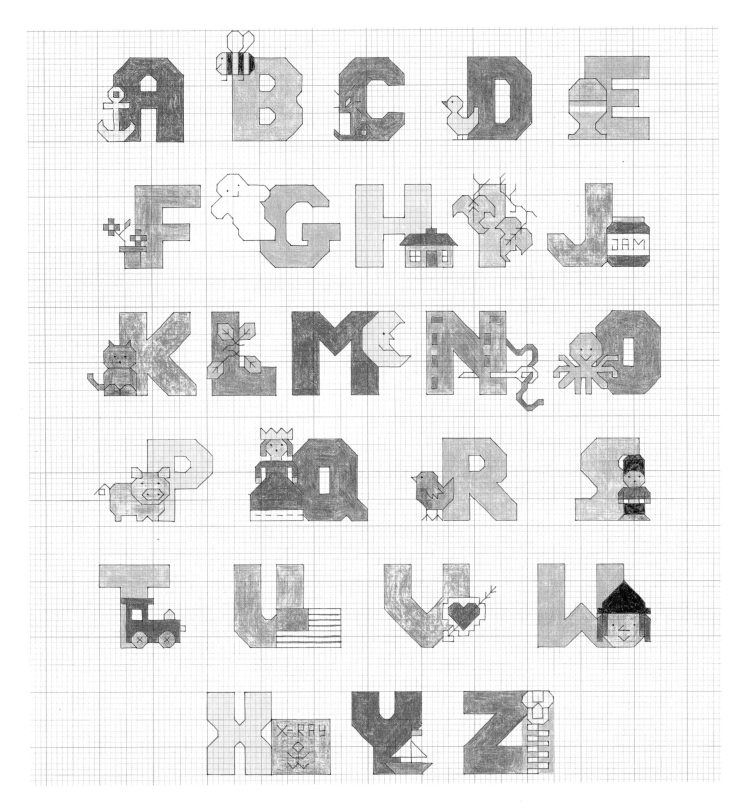

Best Wishes & Thank You

Actions speak louder than words, and if you take the trouble to cross-stitch your message, the recipient will know that you mean what you say.

BEST WISHES

Finished size:

18cm x 12cm (7in x 4¾in)

Inner frame: 14cm x 8cm (5½in x 3⅛in)

You will need:

- 25cm x 15cm (10in x 6in) of white 14-count Aida
- Size 24 tapestry needle
- One skein of each colour listed in the chart
- 18cm x 36cm (7in x 14¼in) coloured cardboard
- Adhesive

NOTE: Outline in black and create the looped border in blue.

	Anchor	DMC		Anchor	DMC		Anchor	DMC
■	403	310	■	101	552	■	239	702
■	25	776	■	146	334	■	28	892

THANK YOU

Finished size:

13cm (5⅛in) square

Inner frame: 9cm (3½in) in diameter

You will need:

• 15-cm (6-in) square of white
14-count Aida

• Size 24 tapestry needle
• One skein of each colour listed in
the chart
• 13cm x 39cm (5⅛in x 15⅜in)
coloured cardboard
• Adhesive

	Anchor	DMC
■	403	310
■	239	702
■	109	209
☐	289	307

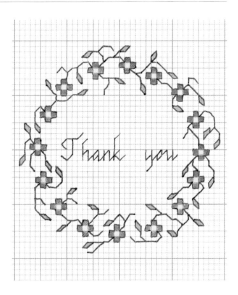

THANK YOU SO MUCH

Finished size:

19.5cm x 11cm (7½in x 4½in)

Inner frame: 15.5cm x 7cm (6¼in x
2¾in)

You will need:

• 25cm x 15cm (10in x 6in) of white
14-count Aida
• Size 24 tapestry needle
• One skein of each colour listed in
the chart
• 19.5cm x 33cm (7½in x 13in)
coloured cardboard
• Adhesive

	Anchor	DMC		Anchor	DMC
■	403	310	■	109	209
■	25	776	☐	239	702
■	101	552			

NOTE: Outline in black

Good Luck

An embroidered card makes a lovely good luck talisman for someone entering an exam, or a similar ordeal.

LUCKY HORSESHOE

You will need:

- 25-cm (10-in) square of white 14-count Aida
- Size 24 tapestry needle
- One skein of each colour listed in the chart
- 14.5cm x 42cm (5¾in x 16½in) coloured cardboard

NOTE: The cat's eyes are created with small French knots. Outline in black.

Finished size:

14.5cm x 14cm (5¾in x 5½in)

Inner frame: 10.5cm x 10cm (4¼in x 4in)

	Anchor	DMC		Anchor	DMC
■	403	310		239	702
	25	776		46	666
	101	552		398	415

GOOD LUCK

Finished size:

17cm x 11.5cm (6¾in x 4½in)

Inner frame: 13cm x 7.5cm (5⅛in x 3in)

You will need:

- 25cm x 20cm (10in x 8in) of white 14-count Aida

- Size 24 tapestry needle
- One skein of each colour listed in the chart
- 17cm x 34.5cm (6¾in x 13½in) coloured cardboard
- Adhesive

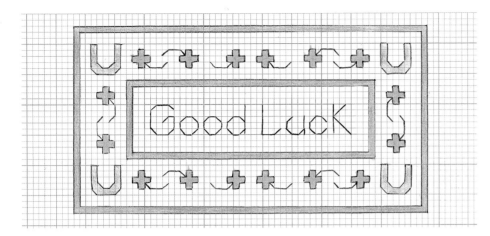

	Anchor	DMC
■	403	310
■	239	702
■	146	334
■	398	415
■	235	414

NOTE: Outline the horseshoes in dark gray and the clover leaves in green.

GOOD LUCK CHARMS

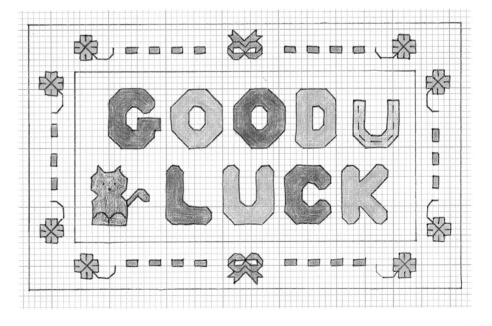

Finished size:

19.5cm x 13cm (7½in x 5⅛in)

Inner frame: 15.5cm x 9cm (6¼in x 3½in)

You will need:

- 25cm x 15cm (10in x 6in) of white 14-count Aida
- Size 24 tapestry needle
- One skein of each colour listed in the chart
- 19.5cm x 39cm (7½in x 15⅜in) coloured cardboard
- Adhesive

NOTE: Outline the letters, clover leaves, cat and horseshoe in black, and the ribbon in deep pink; back-stitch the inner and outer border in deep red.

	Anchor	DMC		Anchor	DMC
■	403	310	■	239	702
■	25	776	■	28	892
■	109	209	■	20	498
■	140	799	■	398	415
■	235	414			

Get Well Wishes

When someone you care for is sick, a cross-stitch card is a delightful way to give them a boost, as it will last much longer than flowers or grapes.

WITH LOVE

- 40cm (16in) of lace, 2cm (³⁄₄in) wide, threaded with 4-mm (¹⁄₈-in) wide pink ribbon
- 4 lilac ribbon roses
- One skein of each colour listed in the chart
- 39cm x 10cm (15³⁄₈in x 4in) coloured cardboard
- Adhesive

NOTE: The bear's eye is created with a small French knot, using black stranded cotton. Outline in black. Assemble the card; attach the white lace trim with craft adhesive, neatly mitring the corners to fit exactly, and finish by glueing a lilac ribbon rose into each corner.

Finished size:
13cm x 10cm (5¹⁄₈in x 4in)
Inner frame: 9cm x 6cm (3¹⁄₂in x 2¹⁄₄in)

You will need:
- 25cm x 20cm (10in x 8in) of white 14-count Aida
- Size 24 tapestry needle

	Anchor	DMC
■	403	310
	347	921
	46	666
□	01	white
	130	809

GET WELL SOON

Finished size:
20cm x 12cm (8in x 4³⁄₄in)
Inner frame: 16cm x 8cm (6¹⁄₄in x 3¹⁄₈in)

You will need:
- 25cm x 15cm (10in x 6in) of white 14-count Aida
- Size 24 tapestry needle

- One skein of each colour listed in the chart
- 20cm x 36cm (8in x 14¹⁄₄in) coloured cardboard
- Adhesive

NOTE: Outline in black.

	Anchor	DMC
	239	702
	25	776
	403	310
	140	799
	101	552
	46	666

WOUNDED BEAR

Finished size:

12cm (4¾in) square

Inner frame: 8cm (3⅛in) square

You will need:

- 15-cm (6-in) square of white 14-count Aida
- Size 24 tapestry needle
- One skein of each colour listed in the chart
- 12cm x 36cm (4¾in x 14⅛in) coloured cardboard
- Adhesive

NOTE: The eyes are made with small French knots, using black stranded cotton. Outline in black.

	Anchor	DMC		Anchor	DMC		Anchor	DMC
	203	954		01	white		347	921
	239	702		403	310		0349	301
	140	799		366	543		371	433

Special Events

A new job, passing a driving test, retirement — all of these are important land-marks, so here is a selection of cheerful cards to add to the excitement.

SORRY YOU'RE LEAVING

Finished size:

15.5cm x 14cm (6¼in x 5½in)

Inner frame: 11.5cm x 10cm (4½in x 4in)

You will need:

- 20-cm (8-in) square of white 14-count Aida
- Size 24 tapestry needle
- One skein of each colour listed in the chart
- 15.5cm x 42cm (6¼in x 16½in) coloured cardboard
- Adhesive

NOTE: The eyes are made with small French knots, using black stranded cotton. Outline in black.

	Anchor	DMC		Anchor	DMC
	347	921		203	954
	367	738		290	444
	0349	301		298	972
	371	433		46	666
	403	310		28	892
	239	702			

CONGRATULATIONS ON PASSING YOUR DRIVING TEST

Finished size:

16cm x 12cm (6¼in x 4¾in)

Inner frame: 12cm x 8cm (4¾in x 3⅛in)

You will need:

- 25cm x 15cm (10in x 6cm) of white 14-count Aida
- Size 24 tapestry needle
- One skein of each colour listed in the chart
- 16cm x 36cm (6¼in x 14¼in) coloured cardboard
- Adhesive

NOTE: Work the cross-stitching first, then the back-stitching. Outline throughout in black.

	Anchor	DMC
■	403	310
■	46	666
■	289	307
■	398	415
□	01	white

New Year

Celebrate a new year, and perhaps an old friendship, with a bright, cheerful card
to set the scene for the future.

HAPPY NEW YEAR

Finished size:

16.5cm x 13cm (6½in x 5⅛in)

Inner frame: 12.5cm x 9cm (5in x
   3½in)

You will need:

• 20-cm (8-in) square of white
   14-count Aida

• Size 24 tapestry needle

• One skein of each colour listed in
   the chart

• 16.5cm x 39cm (6½in x 15⅜in)
   coloured cardboard

• Adhesive

NOTE: Either use the photograph as a
guide or select colours at random
when stitching the stars and party
streamers. Outline in black.

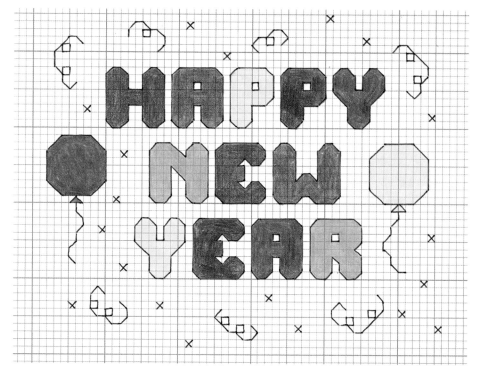

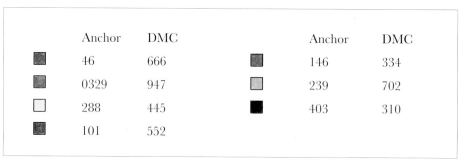

	Anchor	DMC		Anchor	DMC
▨	46	666	▨	146	334
▨	0329	947	▨	239	702
☐	288	445	■	403	310
▨	101	552			

80

AULD LANG SYNE

Finished size:

16.5cm x 17cm (6½in x 6¾in)

Inner frame: 12.5cm x 13cm (5in x 5⅛in)

You will need:

- 25-cm (10-in) square of white 14-count Aida
- Size 24 tapestry needle
- One skein of each colour listed in the chart
- 16.5cm x 51cm (6½in x 20¼in) coloured cardboard
- Adhesive

NOTE: Use the photograph as a guide when selecting colours for the party streamers and stars. Outline the balloons in black. If you prefer to make this card rectangular instead of almost square, set the balloons, stars and party streamers down one or both sides.

	Anchor	DMC		Anchor	DMC
■	403	310	■	28	892
■	146	334	□	288	445
■	239	702	■	298	972
■	255	907	■	101	552
■	46	666	■	109	209

NATIONAL HOLIDAYS

*I*f you have a friend or relative who will be far from home on the relevant day, a cross-stitch card will show that they are not forgotten.

North America

Get into the spirit of the occasion and add some extra sparkle to events; cards as attractive as these should be kept and re-used in future years.

THANKSGIVING

Finished size:

13cm (5⅛in) square

Inner frame: 9cm (3½in) square

You will need:

- 20-cm (8-in) square of white 14-count Aida
- Size 24 tapestry needle
- One skein of each colour listed in the chart
- 13cm x 39cm (5⅛in x 15⅜in) coloured cardboard
- Adhesive

NOTE: Outline in black.

	Anchor	DMC		Anchor	DMC
	403	310		20	498
	239	702		22	815
	229	701		288	445
	255	907		290	444
	46	666		109	209
	0349	301		103	211
	silver thread				

INDEPENDENCE DAY

Finished size:

13.5cm x 18cm (5¼in x 7in)

Inner frame: 9.5cm x 14cm (3½in x 5½in)

You will need:

- 20cm x 30cm (8in x 12in) of white 14-count Aida
- Size 24 tapestry needle
- One skein of each colour listed in the chart
- 40.5cm x 18cm (16in x 7in) coloured cardboard
- Adhesive

NOTE: Outline in black.

	Anchor	DMC			Anchor	DMC
■	403	310		■	146	334
■	48	963		□	01	white
■	46	666				

AMERICA

Finished size:

17cm x 11.5cm (6¾in x 4½in)

Inner frame: 14.5cm x 9cm (5¾in x 3½in)

You will need:

- 25cm x 20cm (10in x 8in) of white 14-count Aida
- Size 24 tapestry needle
- One skein of each colour listed in the chart
- Adhesive

- 17cm x 34.5cm (6¾in x 13½in) coloured cardboard

NOTE: Work the cross-stitching first, then the back-stitching. Outline the hearts, crosses, flags and individual black cross-stitches in black. (For chart and key, see overleaf.)

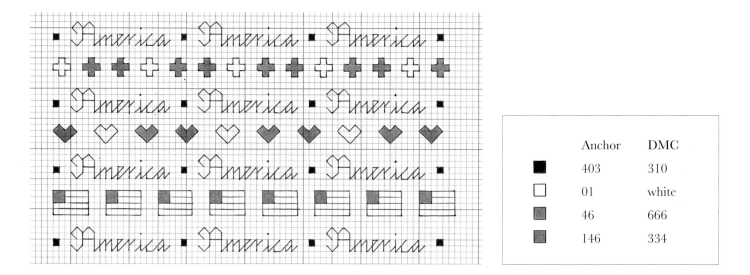

	Anchor	DMC
■	403	310
□	01	white
▨	46	666
▨	146	334

DOMINION DAY

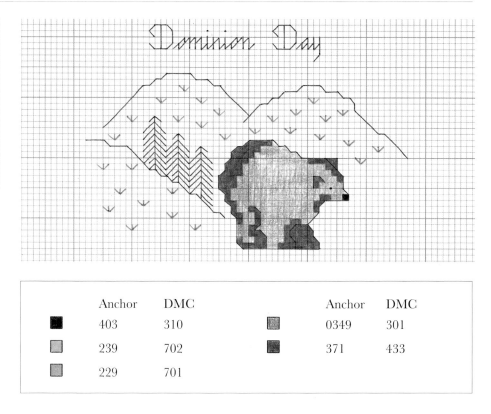

Finished size:

15.5cm x 12cm (6¼in x 4¾in)

Inner frame: 11.5cm x 8cm (4½in x 3⅛in)

You will need:

- 20-cm (8-in) square of white 14-count Aida
- Size 24 tapestry needle
- One skein of each colour listed in the chart
- 15.5cm x 36cm (6¼in x 14¼in) coloured cardboard
- Adhesive

	Anchor	DMC		Anchor	DMC
■	403	310	▨	0349	301
▨	239	702	▨	371	433
▨	229	701			

NOTE: Outline the bear in black and stitch the trees in dark green; all other backstitching is in fresh green.

The British Isles

The British saints' days are celebrated in the next four designs, starting with Saint George and the dragon (the patron saint of England).

ST GEORGE'S DAY

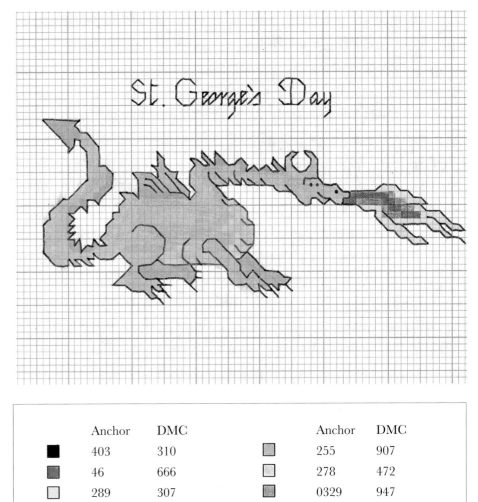

Finished size:

20cm x 13cm (8in x 5⅛in)

Inner frame: 16cm x 9cm (6¼in x 3½in)

You will need:

- 25-cm (10-in) square of white 14-count Aida
- Size 24 tapestry needle
- One skein of each colour listed in the chart
- 20cm x 39cm (8in x 15⅜in) coloured cardboard
- Adhesive

NOTE: The dragon's eyes and nose are made with small French knots, using black stranded cotton. Outline the dragon and flames in black.

	Anchor	DMC		Anchor	DMC
■	403	310	▨	255	907
▧	46	666	▢	278	472
▢	289	307	▨	0329	947
▨	239	702			

ST DAVID'S DAY

Finished size:

12.5cm x 19cm (5in x 7½in)

Inner frame: 8.5cm x 15cm (3¼in x 6in)

You will need:

- 20cm x 25cm (8in x 10in) of white 14-count Aida
- Size 24 tapestry needle
- One skein of each colour listed in the chart
- 37.5cm x 19cm (15in x 7½in) coloured cardboard
- Adhesive

NOTE: Outline the stems, leaves and flowers in black. The stamen is created with eight back-stitches, using black stranded cotton.

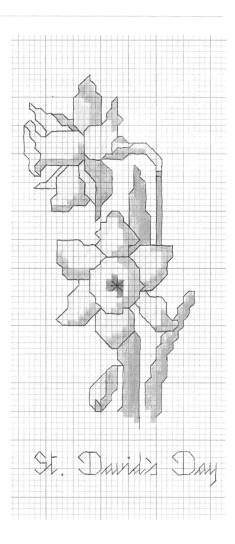

	Anchor	DMC		Anchor	DMC
☐	290	444	■	403	310
☐	298	972	☐	239	702
☐	0329	947	☐	255	907

ST PATRICK'S DAY

Finished size:

10.5cm x 14cm (4¼in x 5½in)

Inner frame: 6.5cm x 10cm (2½in x 4in)

You will need:

- 15cm x 20cm (6in x 8in) of white 14-count Aida
- Size 24 tapestry needle
- One skein of each colour listed in the chart
- 31.5cm x 14cm (12¾in x 5½in) coloured cardboard
- Adhesive

NOTE: Work the cross-stitching first, then the back-stitching. Create the eyes and nose with small French knots, using black stranded cotton. The stripes on the socks are back-stitched in light green. Outline in black.

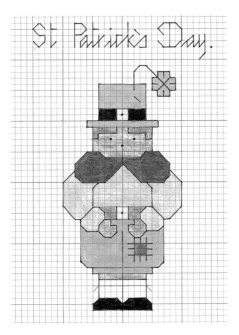

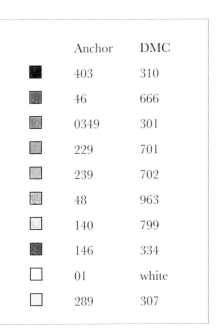

	Anchor	DMC
	403	310
	46	666
	0349	301
	229	701
	239	702
	48	963
	140	799
	146	334
	01	white
	289	307

St Andrew's Day

- Size 24 tapestry needle
- One skein of each colour listed in the chart
- 37.5cm x 15.5cm (15in x 6¼in) coloured cardboard
- Adhesive

Note: For the thistle, use one strand each of the light and dark purple together in the needle. Outline in black.

Finished size:
12.5cm x 15.5cm (5in x 6¼in)
Inner frame: 8.5cm x 11.5cm (3¼in x 4½in)

You will need:
- 20cm x 25cm (8in x 10in) of white 14-count Aida

	Anchor	DMC
	403	310
	229	701
	101	552
	109	209

Australasia

Make a cheering card for someone who is far from home, or perhaps for a rarely-seen grandchild, and shorten the distance between you.

NEW ZEALAND

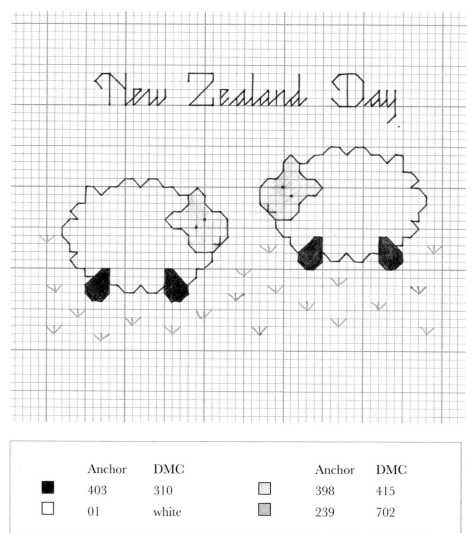

Finished size:

16cm x 12cm (6¼in x 4¾in)

Inner frame: 12cm x 8cm (4¾in x 3⅛in)

You will need:

- 20-cm (8-in) square of white 14-count Aida
- Size 24 tapestry needle
- One skein of each colour listed in the chart
- 16cm x 36cm (6¼in x 14¼in) coloured cardboard
- Adhesive

NOTE: The sheep's eyes are made with small French knots, using black stranded cotton. Outline the sheep in black and use green for the grass.

	Anchor	DMC		Anchor	DMC
■	403	310	▨	398	415
□	01	white	▨	239	702

AUSTRALIA DAY

Finished size:

15cm x 12cm (6in x 4¾in)

Inner frame: 11cm x 8cm (4½in x 3⅛in)

You will need:

- 25cm x 20cm (8in x 10in) of white 14-count Aida
- Size 24 tapestry needle
- Adhesive
- One skein of each colour listed in the chart
- 15cm x 36cm (6in x 14¼in) coloured cardboard

NOTE: Outline the kangaroo, the palm trees, the ship and the boomerang in black stranded cotton; back-stitch Australia in dark blue.

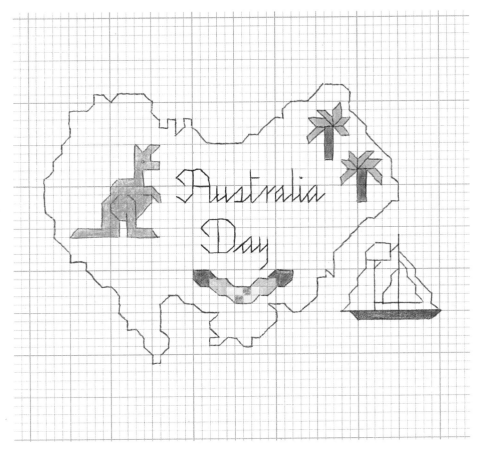

	Anchor	DMC
	01	white
	46	666
	403	310
	239	702
	255	907
	347	921
	290	444
	133	796
	109	209
	0349	301
	140	799

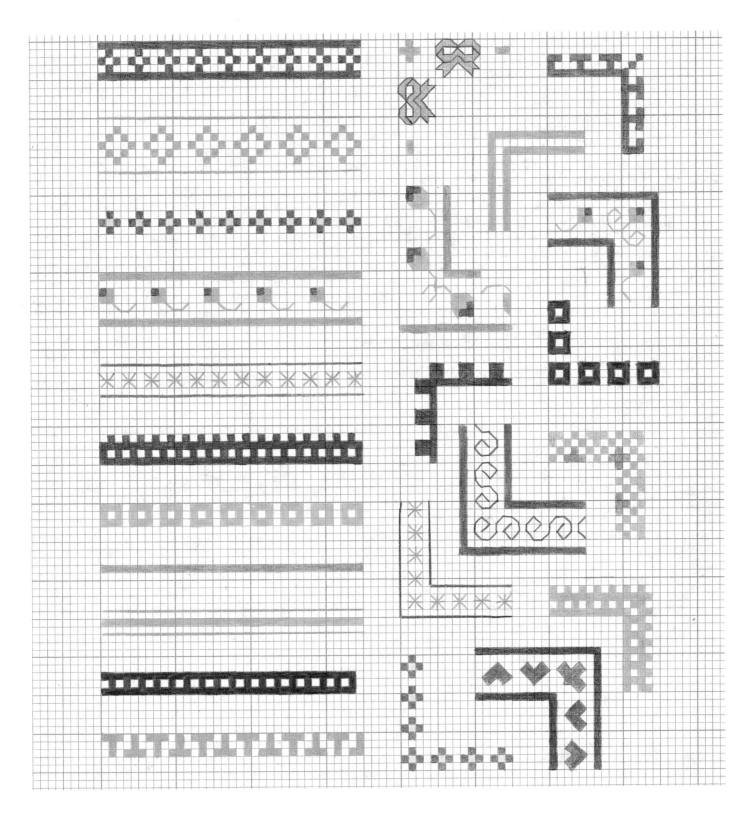

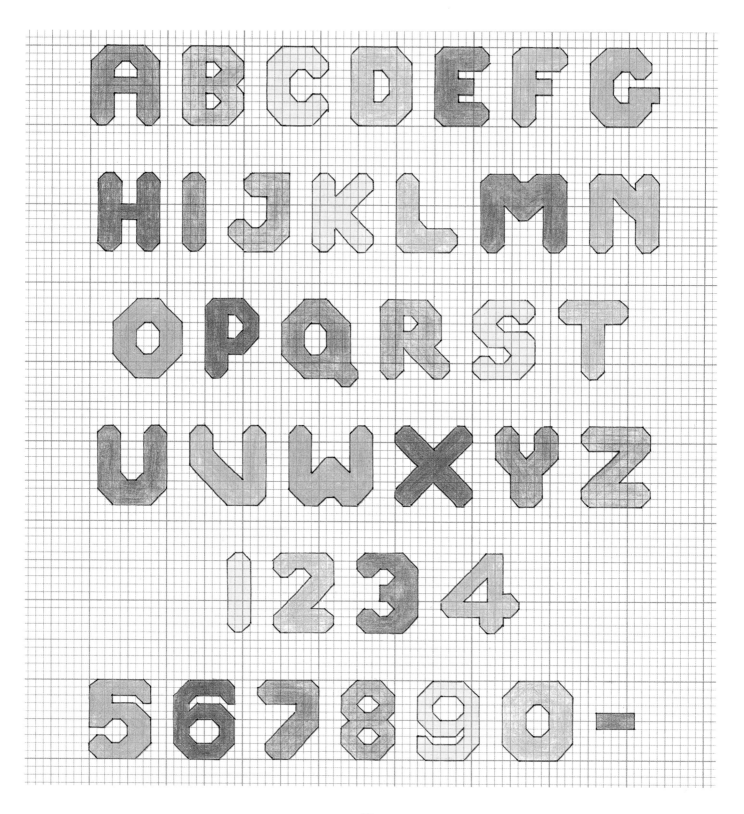

Index

Acknowledgments

The publishers would like to thank the following companies for supplying materials for photography:
The Chelsea Gardener, 125 Sydney Street, London SW3 6NR;
Designer's Guild, 271-277 King's Road, London SW3 5EN;
The Dining Room Shop, 62-64 White Hart Lane, London SW13 UPZ;
Global Village, 247-9 Fulham Road, London SW3;
V.V. Rouleaux, 210 New King's Road, London SW6.